AF413592

THE POWER OF
COURAGE

Sam Glenn

The Authority on Attitude©

Content Based on Sam Glenn's Motivational Speeches

and Training (www.samglenn.com)

ISBN: 978-969-2792-14-1

A Few Words from The Attitude Guy...

While this book may not be hundreds of pages long, it's got a lot of great content, lessons, and valuable ideas on living a more courageous life.

My hope is that the words that fill these pages feed your courage muscle and expand your awareness of how valuable living with courage really is. Sometimes, we need a quick source of encouragement to keep our head up, our focus moving forward, and our mental outlook fueled with grit and resilience. You are about to discover that courage is more than just a seven-letter word. It's how we think, act, and live. Courage is essential, timeless, vital, and relevant to both our personal and professional life. We gotta have it! Bottom line, we need to live with courage every day.

Is it easy? Not always, and that's why I felt compelled to write on this subject.

I am often asked what inspires me, and honestly, I love stories. I love hearing other people's stories because it gives me hope and makes me not feel alone. And in every story,there are great lessons to be learned. So, I thought for this book, I would share a little about my story, history, and the courageous life lessons gained through relationships, work, research, and observation.

I know that you have a story going on in your life right now—it may be at work or at home. Life is always changing, like the seasons, so only you know what part of your life needs a little courage right now.

So, raise your coffee cup as I am, and here is to thinking better, doing better, and living with courage! Enjoy.

Sam Glenn

The Authority on Attitude ©

Table of Contents

1 Life RequiresCourage 1

2 Courage is Not Giving Up on Yourself 6

3 Courage Changes How You See Things 13

4 Courage Gives Us Strength to Face the Unexpected........ 19

5 It Takes Courage to Do the Right Thing........................... 21

6 It Takes Courage to Let Go 26

7 It Takes Courage to Keep Your Cool 31

8 It Takes Courage to Walk Your Talk 38

9 It Takes Courage to Believe What Your Critics Don't..... 45

10 Our Courage Becomes Stronger When We Stick Together

.... 54

11 It Takes Courage to Love Unconditionally...................... 58

12 It Takes Courage to Be Grateful 60

13 It Takes Courage to Put Yourself First 69

14 It Takes Courage to Be Positively Contagious................ 75

15 It Takes Courage to Lead in Life 82

The Wrap Up 87

Meet the Author.. 89

1

Life RequiresCourage

"LIFE REQUIRES COURAGE."

Would you agree with that statement?

When I was researching the topic of courage, the defini- tion that came up the most was: mental or moral strength to persevere and withstand danger, fear, or difficulty.

But let me ask you, how do "YOU" define courage?

Recently, I posted a question on my Facebook page **(@SamGlennSpeaker):**

"What does courage mean to you?"

Every response was slightly different, which led me to believe that we all define courage based on where we need it or want to see it demonstrated the most in our life and at work. The meaning of courage holds a personal and unique value to us all. The act of courage can be inspiring and life-changing. Courage can be an admirable and brave act, SAM GLENN like running into a burning building to save someone, or the person who remains calm in an emergency situation. Courage can be as simple as sharing a few encouraging words with someone feeling down or simply slowing down to be safe when you are in a mad rush. You see, the application of courage is boundless, and when you boil it down, it's evident that LIFE REQUIRES COURAGE.

Think about it, we need courage:

- To keep going when we feel like giving up.

- To make new life choices that take us in a better direction.

- To let go of what is no longer healthy for us.

- To speak up in constructive ways.

- To sit down and listen.

- To lend a helping hand.

- To share our story.

- To pursue a dream.

- To do the right thing.

- To admit when we are wrong.

- To face our fears.

And the list of areas we need and can apply courage to can go on and on. But what does courage mean to you, and where it is the most relevant in your life?

LIFE REQUIRES COURAGE

Take a brief moment to write out the date and what having courage means to you below. (Someday, you may open this book again, and it's always fun to look back on our personal development notes.) Also, by writing this out, it helps clarify and build a stronger awareness of what courage is and what it means to you:

What does courage mean to you:

Courage is:

____

4

____

2

Courage is Not Giving Up on Yourself

Don't ever let anyone turn your sky into a ceiling.

Before I started my professional speaking career 21 years ago, I studied improv at Second City in Chicago, and I was on a mission to get on SNL *(Saturday Night LIVE)* and eventually, into television and movies. That was the goal. In fact, I was even offered a full-time role on a very successful television series where I had been an extra. Sometimes, I would entertain the other extras with my humorous stories and impersonations while waiting around to shoot scenes, and that got me some positive attention from casting directors. It also got me kicked off a few sets. Directors don't like to hear people laughing during serious scenes. But honestly, I didn't mind. Some days, I would work on set for 8-10 hours, get paid $50, and once they took taxes out, I had enough to buy lunch and a ride home. It had its fun moments and was a learning experience, for sure.

However, I passed on the role that was offered to me and for good reason: I just didn't feel it was my calling. I wanted to do something that gave me a deeper sense of purpose. I wanted to do something more meaningful. And who knew it would be the one thing that absolutely scared me the most—public speaking!

Most people assume that public speakers are extroverts with tons of charisma, who love attention and relish in the public eye. Let me just say, that is not the case for me. I am shy by nature and quiet in crowds. I don't like or need all the attention in a room, and it baffles people when they see how reserved, quiet, and laid back I am off the stage.

My first so-called speaking gig was teaching Sunday

school to 100 overly tired and ornery teenagers who had no desire to be at church. I would say it wasn't as much of a gig as it was getting involved and doing something that helped out. It was the path less traveled. Speaking to a crowd of tired teenagers can be scary, and the key is that you can't show fear. If you do, they will eat you up. To say the least, it wasn't a pretty picture I was walking into. I remember thinking, what did I get myself into? Why was I doing this to myself?

NOT GIVING UP ON YOURSELF

It was a challenge from day one to captivate everyone's attention and give them something of valuable substance that they could apply to their everyday lives. My big advantage was that I had, and still have, attention deficit disorder. Some may see it as having a weakness, but I leveraged it and used it as a major strength. Trust me, it's not easy to hold the attention of someone with ADD. If it doesn't dazzle or sparkle, good luck! I think that is one thing that impresses my clients today—my ability to captivate and hold every- one's attention for long periods of time. For real, you just don't see people drifting off, daydreaming, playing on their phone, or looking for an escape plan during my speeches. I credit this ability as turning a weakness into a strength. Plus, I give all parents with ADD children hope.

So, here is when things changed. I had to change my approach because what I was doing wasn't working. One Sunday, I walked up to the front of the room and began shouting out a football cadence like Peyton Manning. It was loud and made no sense at all. Every teenager stopped talking, turned in my direction, and basically gave me a look like I had lost my marbles. However, they were oddly entertained and became engaged to see what I would do next. Let's just say I had to get a little creative to captivate, but it worked. Communication without captivation is a waste of time. There is no retention, and the value of the content is missed.The journey toward my dream of speaking full-time got off to a rocky start. Most Sundays, I left the class feeling like I didn't get through to anyone or that I failed miserably in my communication efforts. Crafting a speech wasn't my strong suit, and I humbly admit that there were a few times I didn't even know what I was talking about. But when you pursue something new, like starting a new business, a new career path, or even a new role in your company, it's not an overnight success story. You must look for what I call mini progress reports. At first, I thought I was failing big time and that my big dream was turning more foolish by the minute. But then I got my first mini progress report. At the end of one class, a young man walked up to me and said, "Mr. Glenn, you should do this every day. I didn't like coming before, but you make it fun. You make us laugh, and what you say really helps me."

That young man's feedback gave me courage to keep going, to keep trying, and to keep getting better.

Eventually, I got another mini progress report—parents started pulling me aside, sharing the same sentiments about their son or daughter. In fact, some parents were so intrigued by the change in their child's attitude and behavior that they wanted to see what I was doing and saying. I began to notice that some parents would actually sneak into the back of my class to observe and listen. I wasn't doing anything magical other than being real, giving my all, and offering positive ways to think better, do better, and live better. In fact, that eventually became the core of what my company is all about today—to empower people and caring organizations to think better, do better, and live better.

Progress feeds our courage. It lets us know we are moving in a positive direction. It eventually transforms into

momentum, which is what we all want! This is why recognition is so valuable and vital in life and the workplace. We want to know we are heading in a positive direction and not just spinning our wheels for nothing. Recognition is the acknowledgement that you are doing the right things with the right attitude. And you may not always get the recognition you merit, but don't let that stop you from recognizing yourself. Don't ever forget to celebrate the small steps you take with big courage. However, even with a little progress and momentum,

it doesn't mean that things become perfect or get easier. It takes courage, mental toughness, and grit to stay the course and keep moving forward. Read on…

3

Courage Changes How You See Things

Failure isn't your tombstone, it's your teacher. It's not a sign to give up, it's a cheerleader to keep going.

My Sunday school class found a positive rhythm and was going really well, but I wanted to start venturing out and sharing my speeches with other groups. So, I took another big step in a direction that scared me—telling the world about my business. It's a process known as marketing, and immediately, I was met with a variety of setbacks and road blocks. I had no money, slept on borrowed floor space when I wasn't working the graveyard shift doing odd jobs, and drove an '82 Buick Regal with a really bad attitude. On paper at first glance, I was in no position to pursue my dream of becoming a world-class motivational speaker. NONE! I had no experience, no contacts, no resume, no pipeline, no physical address, no marketing budget, no marketing skills, and no idea where to start. I was honestly scared out of my mind at this point. It may sound humorous, but with all the doubt and fear I had bouncing around in my mind, I really thought there would be a legitimate chance I would end up living in a van down by the river next to Matt Foley. (SNL reference.)

Looking back, one lesson that is extremely vivid and stays with me to this day is when I focused on my doubts, felt sorry for myself, complained, blamed, or worried about why it couldn't be done. I would get lazy and think, "What's the point?"

On those days, I didn't do much, and nothing great was accomplished. My choices defeated me. This is why courage is so vital to our way of thinking. When you minimize your courageous thinking, you focus on and feed more of your doubts, fears, and stress. That is not a happy or productive picture for anyone.

Surprisingly, it was in those difficult moments that I would stumble upon some enlightening words in a book, a positive quote, or someone who was willing to share a little bit of their courage with me. All of those things gave me courage to keep going. I discovered that having a sense of courage altered my negative perspectives. I saw things differently. I realized the unpaved road wasn't there to stop me or slow me down from reaching my goals, but was simply part of the preparation process for the bigger picture of who I am and what I do today. When my thinking lacked courage, I would complain about why things couldn't just be easier. It reminds me of a quote by the late Jim Rohn: "Don't wish things were easier, wish you were better. Don't wish for less problems, wish for more skills. Don't wish for less challenge, wish for more wisdom." When my thinking was fueled by courage, road blocks and setbacks dramatically changed in appearance. I didn't view them as blocking me from success, but rather, as learning opportunities, valuable education, and building blocks to get to where I wanted to go. Having a little courage mixed into my thinking also helped me sleep better. That may not sound like a big deal to some, but in my opinion, there is nothing worse than going to bed with a mind that is filled with anxiety,

fear, and doubt. It makes for a very restless and long night.

Courage filled my mind with comfort, confidence, hope, motivation, purpose, belief, excitement, expectation, and resilience. I made sure that before I closed my eyes, my courage was bigger and louder than my fears, doubts, and anxiety. I read uplifting books and listened to great speeches on cassette tapes. Yeah—cassette tapes. That's how far back this story goes.

Eventually, I got to this point on my journey—the

present. This isn't my final destination but rather, part of the journey. Even though I have been going full-steam for 21 years, every day still requires courage. But think of it this way: if I had subscribed to my doubts, fears, and anxieties, you would not be reading these words right now. How powerful is that???!!!! With a little courage, you can write beautiful stories into your life. Sometimes, before you get to the beauty part, things go through a few messy stages, but with courage, you are confident that great things are possible for you.

The big takeaway here is that courage is determined by how we think. We need to feed our thinking with what gives our courage life. Courage takes the hand of our attitude and behavior and gives us the strength to take a small step in a direction we thought we had no ability to go.

Having the courage to believe in yourself is not being blind to your imperfections or weaknesses but rather, taking things in stride and giving more acknowledgment to your strengths. Having courage is facing your limitations with the right attitude and not letting them hold you back.

Courage is the recognition that we are not perfect, but we have the power and ability to get up and get a little better every day. Getting a little better every day is what feeds progress and creates positive momentum in your life.

COURAGE CHANGES HOW YOU SEE THINGS

Remember, you have nothing to lose by believing in the greatness of who you are, and you have everything to gain when you do. Here is another favorite quote of mine: "Anyone can give up, it's the easiest thing in the world to do. But to hold it together when everyone else would understand if you fell apart, that's true strength."

Keep going…

4

Courage Gives Us Strength to Face the Unexpected

Adversity doesn't make appointments, does it? The other day, I finished speaking at a leadership meeting for an outstanding organization, who just received the honor of being named one of the Best Places to Work. It takes a lot of work and caring people to achieve that honor. As I was cleaning up from my performance painting, the president of the company came up and quietly shared a little bit of his story.

"Sam, first, I want to thank you for your words today. I needed them more than you know. I waited for everyone to leave because I didn't want anyone to find out that I was recently diagnosed with advanced prostate cancer. I have heard speeches and read books on attitude my whole life, but it has never held as much meaning as it does right now. I am a dad and a husband, and I am not ready to go yet. Some days, I feel scared because I don't know what to expect, and other days, I feel strong because I have amazing people who give me strength. When my wife grabs my hand and whispers, 'It's all going to be okay,' I feel courage to keep fighting. After hearing you speak today, I know one thing for sure: cancer will not win. There is the possibility it may take my life, but it will not beat me. I will beat this in how I approach it—with my attitude. I will be an example for my kids and others going through the same thing. I know it won't be easy, but when you have the strength of others, you can do so much more than you ever thought. I choose not to give up."

And I am going to end this chapter right there. His insightful words summed it up perfectly.

5

It Takes Courage to Do the Right Thing

I recently read a story about a woman who rode her bike to the store to run a quick errand. When she came out, her bike was stolen. The next day, she had a hunch and glanced on Craigslist to see if anyone was trying to sell her bike, and sure enough—there it was for sale!

Not letting the buyer know who she was, she inquired about the bike and scheduled a public meeting at McDonalds to see if it was, in fact, her bike. And sure enough—it was! She smiled and asked the seller if she could give it a test ride. The guy said, "Sure, but just don't ride off with it."

And just like that, she rode off into the sunset, and they

never saw each other again. The story ends up being a vic- tory for her, but what it also communicates is that when you choose to act with a lack of integrity, in the end, you lose. A lack of integrity is a pathway for loss. One thing is for sure—our integrity will always be put to the test.

I believe integrity is essential in the little things. And it's not just about having integrity with others, but also with ourselves. When I started working on improving my health, I remember going for coffee in the morning, and I could smell the freshly baked donuts at the donut shop. The temptation was unbearable at times. I had a very intense debate going on in my mind. It was a debate that involved integrity. At first, I thought, *Maybe I will get one donut, and nobody will know.* Or maybe, *I will just eat one donut instead of three, and that will be a good thing.* If you are debating integrity in your mind, it's probably not going to lead to a positive result. A lack of integrity is a lack of integrity. Ask yourself, what is the right thing to do? And then do it.

On the flip side, I knew if I cheated on my diet plan, then I would just be hurting myself. It would also be hurting my family because I would feel sluggish and probably moody from all the sugar. The bottom line is that I would be losing integrity with myself and those I care about. When you weigh the consequences of not practicing integrity, you realize that it's just not worth it.

DO THE RIGHT THING

A lack of integrity is a loss for everyone.

It takes courage to do the right things. It takes courage to follow through on your word. It takes courage to take ownership and not blame others when you mess up. Integrity plays a huge role in the little choices we make daily. It shows up in the little things we do, like how we treat others, how we do our work, how we manage our responsibilities, and how we use our time. It takes courage to be real with yourself and do the right thing. When you become consistent with your integrity, you are awarded one of the greatest things ever—TRUST. Trust is the pathway to great relationships, business, health, wealth, and so much more. Trust is a gift that can only be given through the act of consistent integrity.

6

It Takes Courage to Let Go

Have you ever had one of those major "WE ARE CLEANING EVERYTHING" weekends? We recently did, and let me just say, sometimes you don't realize how much junk there is until you focus on removing it.

We had just gotten home from vacation and missed two weeks of garbage pick-up service, so the trash I took out before we left for our trip began to smell—badly. When you throw out milk or leftovers before you travel and leave it sitting in a warm garage, the smell can turn toxic.

Our clean-up weekend expanded into a full, week-long project. It was time to let things go, clean out the clutter, and toss out what needed to go. The bags of trash, old furniture, and odd stuff began piling up in our garage. At first, it was manageable, but after the fourth day, there was so much trash you couldn't even walk around. I remember thinking, "Where did all this trash come from?"

And let me just say, when garbage sits around for a long period of time, it doesn't turn into a tropical air freshener. All the trash I put out before vacation was stinking up everything. The smell was attaching itself to anything it could. A good lesson to interject here is: Attitudes are contagious. Remove the stink before the stink attaches itself to everything and everyone and stinks up everything. That may sound a little corny or cheesy, but it's the truth. When has a sour attitude ever made life sweeter? It doesn't. So, don't let it grow and gain strength. At one point, the smell of the garbage was so strong in my garage, I told my wife, "Umm, I think we should move."

Instead, I called a same-day garbage removal company. After they removed everything, we had freedom again. We had space to move around and breathe. It was like a huge weight was lifted! And best of all, the debilitating smell was gone. We could take off our gas masks.

IT TAKES COURAGE TO LET GO

The moral of the story is that sometimes we need to do a little mental clean up, and get rid of the garbage or clutter we collect in our mind over time. It takes courage to let go and move forward. Maybe it was a bad experience you had growing up, a relationship that wasn't healthy, workplace drama…it could be anything. It takes courage to clean it all up. That may involve allowing yourself to recover and heal. Or perhaps, it's a way of thinking that that doesn't serve you anymore, and it's taking up too much space. It's time to let it go, clean things up, and move on. It's time to do it with courage. When we let the garbage and trash build up in our mind, it begins to stink up our attitude and behavior. That's all it does—stinks things up for us. Mental trash overflow can show up in how we treat others and ourselves. If you let the trash build up too much, there won't be any room for the good stuff. You will be living a life with limitations.

The process of letting go, moving on, and changing what needs to be changed takes courage. It takes courage to stop ignoring the trash and remove it once and for all. For a very long time in my life—years, in fact—I always thought of myself as worthless. I am not sure where the root of that started, but I never felt good enough. Even when I accomplished great things, they didn't seem credible to me because of my thinking. Basically, I was allowing a trash-filled thought to stink up my attitude, and it showed up in my reality. Instead of believing I could make a positive contribution, I felt like what I did didn't matter. I needed to remove the trash-filled belief and find a healthier way of thinking that worked in my favor. Eventually, I took out the trash on this way of thinking, and I feel more freedom and value than I ever have. Make sense?

When you get rid of the mental trash that holds you back, you will feel like an incredible weight has been lifted. This process may take a little time and involve creating some new boundaries and structure, sitting down with someone who can help you sort your thoughts out, or perhaps, it's declaring ENOUGH IS ENOUGH. A courageous step in the right direction is you building new momentum and direction for your way of thinking. And that's a very good thing. You are worth it. Don't ever forget that.

The moment you get rid of the trash in your mind and dump it, you will begin to experience a better you who thinks better, does better, and lives better.

7

It Takes Courage to Keep Your Cool

STRESS! And MORE STRESS!

What stresses you out? How do you manage your stress? Have you ever had so much stress that you just had no sense of calmness? Has stress ever pushed you to do something you knew wasn't healthy for you— like overeat, drink, or binge-watch Netflix for days?

Have you ever just lost your cool and thought, "That wasn't good. I need to find a better way to relax or a better way of responding to things."

Too much of the wrong kind of stress can accumulate and steal our sense of peace. Personally, I feel if it steals your peace, then it's not worth it. The great news is that you have a say in the process of how you manage and deal with stress in your life. There are some really good ways to manage negative stress so it doesn't create negative experiences or alter your health.

When stress builds up and becomes unmanaged, it can affect our health in serious ways. It can cause overwhelming anxiety, stomachaches, fatigue, headaches, rashes, knots in your back, bad breath, illness, and high blood pressure. There are a mess of things that can go wrong if you ignore unmanaged stress. It can even lead to spontaneous bouts of anger or depression. Again, the great news is that you have a say in how you manage your stress.

Recently, I pinched a nerve in the upper left part of my chest. It didn't feel good at all. However, the location of this pain and the pressure I was feeling gave the impression of a different story. Being closer to the age of 50 and having pains in that area of the chest might give the impression of a heart attack. So, to be safe and give my wife comfort, I went to the cardiovascular emergency center. The level of speed, communication, and teamwork was beyond impressive. There is no waiting room at that place and for good reason.

IT TAKES COURAGE TO KEEP YOUR COOL

Within minutes, they had me hooked up to wires and had an IV in my arm. I was flat on my back, and they were calmly working to pinpoint the cause of the pain so they could help me. What amazed me the most was how calm they were in an emergency situation. I mean, it was beyond impressive. Despite all the activity going on, their attitudes actually made me feel calmer. If anyone says attitude doesn't make a difference, they are wrong. It makes a HUGE DIFFERENCE!

After seven hours on a gurney, everything came back normal. My heart was fine. It was just a pinched nerve in the wrong place. However, I had seven hours to lay there and just think. I am not going to lie, it was scary being there. But I started to think, there is nothing worth giving yourself a heart attack over. Nothing. It reiterates the point that if something or a situation is zapping your peace, then it's not worth it. It really isn't. And it takes courage to keep your cool and remain calm in a situation that is clearly zapping you of your peace. Would you agree with that?

I admit, there are moments when I have let little things get to me. So, it's something I acknowledge that I need to work on. We work on getting better at something through practice and awareness. Is it easy? Nope. Does it require some courage? Yep.

I used to get worked up if someone parked too close to my car, getting bad service, slow internet, long lines, too much to do, lost keys, a messy office, and the list goes on. It's those little things that can build up and fuel negative stress. That kind of stress can affect our emotional management skills, causing us to be overly reactive or sensitive to something minor. As a result, we may do or say something without any filter or regard to the consequence. And some- times, our stress can be multiplied when someone gives us some of their stress. That's called someone having a bad day and making sure you share the same vibe.

Remaining calm requires practice. And as long as you have a beating heart and air pumping through your lungs, there will never be a shortage of opportunities to practice keeping your cool. When you feel anxiety or anger coming on, you have to shift your thinking quickly. Focus on your breathing and relax. Shift your thinking to something that grounds you to a place of calmness—it can be thinking about someone you love, something you are grateful for, or something that makes you laugh. The next time you feel yourself getting worked up, and it feels like everything is turning negative, including your attitude and choices—practice these three strategies for managing your stress immediately:

1. Shift your thinking to something that calms you.

2. Remember and repeat this little statement,

"NOTHING is worth having a heart attack over."

3. Do something that releases the stress—go for a walk, walk away from the situation or person for a few minutes, or go outside and take some deep breaths.

4. Do something that helps you regain a healthy sense of calmness.

When I walked out of the emergency cardiovascular center, my nurse pulled me aside and said, "Sam, you are one of the lucky ones today. You get to go home. Be grateful for that."

I AM!

Even though it was only a pinched nerve, it was an eye-opening experience for me. It made me realize that I need to slow down and not take everything so seriously. It takes courage to stay calm when everything is making you feel unhinged. It takes courage to practice what works and helps, so refer to the three strategies above as a starting point to managing unmanaged stress, and you will see a big difference in how you think, feel, and respond to the little things.

8

It Takes Courage to Walk Your Talk

A man was being tailgated by a stressed-out woman at a busy intersection. Suddenly, the light changed. However, several people were still crossing the street, so the man waited with patience. The tailgating woman was furious and honked her horn, screaming in frustration as she missed her chance to get through the intersection.

As she was still in mid-rant, she heard a tap on her window and looked up into the face of a very serious police officer. The officer ordered her to exit her car with her hands up. He took her to the police station, where she was searched, fingerprinted, photographed, and placed in a holding cell. After a couple of hours, a policeman approached the cell and opened the door. She was escorted back to the booking desk where the arresting officer was waiting with her personal effects.

He said, "I'm very sorry for the mistake. You see, I pulled up behind your car while you were blowing your horn, flip- ping off the guy in front of you and cussing a blue streak at him. I noticed the 'What Would Jesus Do' bumper sticker, the 'Choose Life' license plate holder, and the 'I AM A SAM GLENN SUPER FAN' bumper sticker. Naturally, I assumed you had stolen the car."

The moral of the story is that your attitude is always on display, and it communicates who you are and what you are about. We are all going to have our off days when we are in a rush or trying to get a million things done, and everyone around us is moving to a different beat. However, if our message does not align with our attitude and behavior, then our message won't hold water.

IT TAKES COURAGE TO WALK YOUR TALK

This chapter follows in line with the chapter on doing the right thing. I am not sure who coined the phrase, "Walk Your Talk," but I like it and live by it. It simply means that you need to align your attitude and behavior with your words. I heard a saying years ago: the fastest way to lose trust is to walk right and talk left. That simply means if you are saying one thing and doing another, then people can't trust you. Your message becomes unbelievable. The key is to develop the mindfulness and awareness that your attitude and actions are always being showcased to the world.

Years ago, I remember checking in some bags at the air- port, and when I got into the security line, one of the security people randomly picked me out and said my bag was too big and that I needed to check it. It really wasn't—not even close, which was very odd. Everyone around me had similarly sized bags or larger, which made it seem like someone was playing a joke on me. As it turns out, it was just someone having a very bad morning, and they decided to share their bad morning with me. I was a target for their venom. I contested their request and insisted that it was the same as everyone else's bag size. This person would not budge and started to abuse their authority by speaking loudly at me with threats of arresting me. And mind you, I was calm and communicating in a very calm tone. In no way was I trying to escalate things, but any reasoning I communicated only set this person off more.

This particular security person was rude, loud, unkind, wouldn't listen, pushy, and unreasonable. It was kind of a no-win situation for me. At that point, I began to feel my blood starting to boil. My muscles tightened in my neck, and my skin started to turn green. Yep, I could feel the HULK coming to life within me. As I was about to HULK OUT, I heard someone ten people back in line shout toward me, "YOU GO, ATTITUDE GUY!"

It was sobering to realize that people who had just seen

me speak at major conference were waiting in line and observing me in action. Had I turned green, my message they heard at their event would become void and worthless. Setting an example that others will follow and trust is making sure your words, actions, and message are aligned. As hard as it was, I kept my cool, got out of line, and proceeded to go check my bag. I can't say the smile on my face was very real, but nevertheless, I smiled as I walked away. It was embarrassing, humbling, and frustrating.

As I was walking past everyone in line, a woman who had just seen me speak a few hours earlier said, "Sam, great message today! And I don't mean the one earlier."

She observed that my attitude was being put to the test by someone who was trying to poison others with their attitude, but the fact that I remained calm and kept the peace made my message more real to them. It was an example that would serve beyond the moment. We are all going to have days that are less than ideal, but with a little courage, you can stay on a good path and walk

your talk. Keep working at it.

9

It Takes Courage to Believe What Your Critics Don't

One day, as a small child, Thomas Edison came home from school and gave a paper to his mother. He said to her, "Mom, my teacher gave me this paper and told me only you are to read it. What does it say?"

Her eyes swelled with tears as she read the letter out loud to her child…

It says, "Your son is a genius. This school is too small for him and doesn't have good enough teachers to train him. Please, teach him yourself."

His mother did just that, until she fell ill and passed away. Many years later, after Edison's mother died, he became one of the greatest inventors of the century.

One day, he was going through some of her things and discovered the letter that his teacher wrote many years before to bring home for his mother. He opened it, and the message written on the letter said, "Your son is mentally deficient. We cannot let him attend our school anymore. He is expelled."

Edison become emotional reading it and then wrote in his diary, "Thomas A. Edison was a mentally deficient child whose mother turned him into the genius of the Century." In life, we encounter people who doubt us, drain us, turn on us and make us feel defeated. They criticize who we are, how we do things, our ideas, our ambitions, the way we look, how we parent, what we spend our money on, our way of thinking, and even our best efforts. Have you ever experienced that? If you have, you probably agree that it takes courage to not listen to your critics and believe what they believe and say. And then there are those who may share constructive criticism with you because they care about you and want you to do better and be better.

They are not critics. They are people in your corner rooting for your success with no judgement. If someone is attempting to tear you down and lessen the value of who you are, they are critics and do not deserve your time or your ear.

When I was in seventh grade, I tried out for the basketball team. I made the team because I was tall, and that was it. I admit, I wasn't good at all. I just wasn't. Instead of encouraging me or trying to help me become better, my teammates made fun of me every day. I remember one game, there was one minute left in the game, and we were up by enough that our coach deemed it safe to put in the last string players. It was my first time on the court getting real action. I was so excited. And with 45 seconds left in regulation, I stole the ball from the other team. It was near mid court, and since I didn't know how to dribble, I dribbled the ball like I was trying to bounce it over my head and into the stands. I tried to do the best I could, but it looked a little foolish because I was bouncing the ball higher than my head at a full sprint. When I looked over at my teammates sitting on the bench, they were all laughing and pointing at me. When I glanced over at my coach, he was laughing but tried to hide it. What was supposed to be a great moment wasn't. It didn't feel good being laughed at like that. I love to laugh, but laughing at others in a negative way is not good for anyone.

When I started basketball, it was with a spirit of fun. But then it became something I didn't look forward to because I was just a warm body taking up space and a target for everyone to make fun of.

One day, one of the really good players came up to me and said, "Sam, you should think about quitting. You are making us all look bad."

The next day, instead of going to practice, I rode the bus home. I didn't know how I was going to tell my parents I quit the basketball team. As soon as I walked in the door, it surprised my mom. She was like,

"What's wrong?!!"

I said, "Everything is fine, but I quit the basketball team. Do we have any Little Debbie snacks? I could use one and maybe some string cheese."

If you have ever watched the hit television show The Goldbergs, then you will be able to picture the next scene from this story. Looking back, it makes me laugh, but at the time, it wasn't Goldbergs funny. My Mom did not accept my resignation from the basketball team. She said, "No way!" and then grabbed me by my jacket to drive me back to practice. We sat in the car outside the school, fighting about going back into practice. I wasn't prepared to budge. Then, my mom shared some motivational insights. "Samuel, I love you, and I know this isn't easy for you. But you can get better and become better than everyone making fun of you. It takes time and work. I believe in you, and you need to believe in yourself and ignore all the bad stuff everyone tells you. Now, get your BUTT OUT OF THE CAR BEFORE I DRAG YOU

IN THERE MYSELF!"

BELIEVE WHAT YOUR CRITICS DON'T

I still didn't get out of the car. That's when she got out and began to walk around to pull me out. This was before remote locks on cars, so I just locked all the doors. Now, it was Goldberg funny. Mom actually started laughing at one point. She was calm and gave the perception that I had won my case and that we would just go home. IT WAS A TRAP! When I unlocked the doors, she grabbed me and began hauling me into the school building. I remember thinking, *I might need therapy one day because of this.* When you are that age, being seen with your parents around other kids your age can really mess you up. Having your mom drag you into school, well, that's just a whole new level. Basically, Mom just didn't want me to quit. She didn't want me to believe the untruthful and hurtful things other people were saying.

We didn't have a lot of extra money back then, and I remember the only way we could afford my basketball shoes was by counting out pennies from the change jar on the living room floor. I felt bad for putting that kind of stress on my parents and then wanting to quit. Basically, I tried to get through the rest of the year and do the best I could. It wasn't easy, but that summer, my dad bought us a basketball hoop for the driveway. Let's just say that by the time we moved, we—my brothers and I—went through three basketball hoops. We played so much, we beat them up with wear and tear. We would play until dark, then turn on the floodlights and keep playing. Eventually, I got a little better, and the better I got, the quieter my critics became. However, it was a process of courage. I could have listened to everyone who made fun of me, but I didn't. It takes courage to do that.

Eventually, my basketball skills did improve to the point of being offered a full-ride basketball scholarship. Oh, and I should mention that every one of my critics was either not playing anymore because they quit or were sitting on the farthest end of the bench. The extra moral here is that when you spend more time making fun of others than working on bettering yourself, you forfeit the rewards of progress, improvement, and achievement.

We are not going to please everyone all the time, and to try is the fastest formula for madness. Critics are people who spend too much time judging others when they should be working on themselves. If someone tries to recruit you into their misery like it's a full-time job, don't join their team. It's a team of unhappiness. Instead, be the better example. Have the courage to believe what your critics won't.

10

Our Courage Becomes Stronger When We Stick Together

Let's be real, life is filled with unexpected detours and bumps in the road. Life's curveballs are inconvenient, uncomfortable, and often draining. Without permission, adversity attacks our attitude and invades our emotions with stress, frustration, confusion, depression, doubt, and fear. However, we don't have to go through the storms of life alone. The thing with courage is that it's a give and take kind of thing. Sometimes, we need it, and other times, we give it. I remember a guy visiting with me after one of my speeches and sharing a picture of his daughter who had passed away many years before in a fatal car accident. Being a father of three, I wondered in my mind, "How is this guy even standing?"

That was my perspective because I don't know that I would be able to function with a life experience like that. However, as I listened more, he said that his courage to get up each day and keep going was finding purpose in what happened. He now helps young people become more aware of the consequences of their choices.

Sometimes, lending others our courage is as simple as just sitting with them and not saying anything. It's just listening. Maybe it's a little empathy or a few uplifting words. I remember my brother sharing a story about his mentor, the late and great chalk artist Bill Leach. Ben recounts that Bill was bedridden with a serious illness that required 24-hour medical supervision. Friends and family would visit Bill, but before anyone would leave, Bill would ask everyone the same question. "Is there anything I can do for you?"

When he asked my brother this question, Ben replied

to Bill, "What can you do? You are sick in bed."

He looked at Ben, smiled, and said, "I can pray for you… how would that be?"

At work or at home, when we stick together and work together, we find incredible strength in each other. Some days, we need it, and other days, we give it. That is what teamwork is all about. Never be afraid to ask for it, either. If you need courage, ask for it. Find the best courage that refuels, recharges, and refocuses your thinking. Asking for strength in others is not weakness. It's an act of courage. It's called being human and having a desire to keep going. Find your family or tribe where you feel safe to be human and true to yourself. When you stick together, you find the strength of courage to face change together. When we stick together, we find compassion, hope, motivation, and what- ever we need to keep moving forward. That is the power of sticking together.

11

It Takes Courage to Love Unconditionally

There was a family of four, a 9-year-old daughter, Lisa, and a 5-year-old son, Mark. Lisa was diagnosed with a rare blood disease and was predicted to die soon if the doctors did not find a cure, which was some amount of blood matching their requirements, likely to be found in blood relatives. Upon testing immediate relatives, it was found that Mark's blood was a compatible match.

Mark was asked by his parents if he would agree to give Lisa his blood. Mark asked, "Will it save Lisa?" When they said yes, he agreed. Two days later, the process of the blood transfer began. Mark was placed on a bed next to Lisa's, and the doctors began to extract his blood.

After some time, Mark began feeling dizzy and asked the doctors if this was the time he would start dying. The doctors were perplexed by his question and discovered Mark never knew the amount of blood required to cure Lisa. He thought all of his blood was needed, and still, he had reluctantly agreed to it. THATS TRUE COURAGE!!!!!

12

It Takes Courage to Be Grateful

If there is one quality that truly displays the measure of a person's core, its how much they express gratitude. Personally, I think its hands down the most impressive quality of a person in business and life. I was always raised to tell people, "Thank you," even if it was for something little. The rule was to expect nothing, and be grateful for everything. One of my greatest observations in life is that people who express gratitude the most are happier people. They just are. I am in awe when I see someone who seems down to nothing, and yet they can still find something to be grateful for. Doesn't that impress you? For real, isn't that just one of the most impressive character qualities a person can have? It takes real courage to express and choose gratitude when you might have a mountain of things to complain about.

Here is an example from my world. Because I am self-employed, there are not a lot of suitable health insurance options that meet my family's needs. When we finally settled on a plan, the monthly expense amounted to some- where between sitting on a Godzilla-sized thumb tack and stubbing your toe ten times a day. Ouch! That may seem like an over exaggeration, but trust me—it's not. That is me putting it mildly.

In fact, after I regained consciousness when my wife first told me how much we were paying monthly, the first thing I did was resort to complaining. It just seemed like the natural thing to do in the moment. I complained about the system, I blamed the government, and I ranted. Did it solve anything? Not at all. Did it annoy everyone? Sure did. Did I feel better? Not much. And that is nature of the subject. How do you respond when things don't seem like they are going your way? Interestingly enough, a short time ago, my wife and I were discussing how grateful we are that we have the insurance. After we brought our newborn son home and after my trip to the emergency room, I glanced at the invoices and nearly passed out again. My wife said to me, "Sam, aren't you now grateful for the insurance? The bills are covered, and you

don't need to worry."

IT TAKES COURAGE TO BE GRATEFUL

Sometimes, it takes a little perspective to see the beauty in a mess. And yes, I am very grateful. As a father and husband, my primary goal is to make sure my family is protected, so yes, I am grateful for the insurance. It doesn't mean I like the situation, but I am able to find the good in it, and that is what matters most.

While this is only one example, I think that many times, it's easy to focus on what is bad about a situation or who is to blame. Have you ever noticed that the more we complain about something, the easier it is to get worked up and sour about things?

It takes courage to be grateful in moments that don't seem ideal. Would you agree?

Years ago, I was sitting with a friend having coffee, and I was literally so broke, I couldn't pay for my coffee. I was walking around parking lots looking for loose change before we met. I didn't want to admit that I didn't even have a dollar to my name. It was such a helpless feeling. I felt bad about my situation, my failures, my mess ups, and where I was in life. I had resorted to being negative about everything, looked for the negative in my circumstances, and expected the negative. Sadly, it was an attitude that didn't work well for me. It's an attitude that wouldn't work well for anyone, anywhere, at any time.

As I sat with my friend over that cup of coffee, which he paid for, I remember talking about how bad my life was for nearly thirty minutes. I could have kept going, but I needed a restroom break. When I got back to our table, I noticed my friend had some paper and a pen sitting in front of him. I inquired what it was for, and he smiled and began to ask me a series of questions that would redirect my attitude.

"Sam, do you have a place to sleep tonight?" "Do you have people who love you?"

"Do you have clothes to wear?"

He asked about twenty or so questions, and I answered them all with a positive "YES." When we finished, he handed me the paper and said, "I don't know about you, but it looks like you have it really good. You have more to be grateful for than you know."

He was right. I was so focused on all that was wrong that I was missing all that was right.

I think we all experience moments at life and work that give us a reason to complain or not feel the most positive. Would you agree with that?

However, if we feed our focus the wrong perspective, we will stew in negative thinking. We will actually weaken our resilience and ability to move forward with the right attitude. We will continue to hunt for more things that are wrong. But when we focus on gratitude, we find it, and it fuels our attitude with strength, hope, resilience, and power.

IT TAKES COURAGE TO BE GRATEFUL

I have to remind myself of this principle often. But it does work. There may be days when you feel down to nothing, but if you can summon the courage to find something to be grateful for, you will discover you aren't that far down, and things aren't as bad as your worry, anger, or frustration would have you believe.

Years ago, when I was around 12 years old, my brothers and I got to pick out one toy at the toy store. The rule was that it had to be under $5. Since this was something that didn't happen often, it was the best day ever. We all picked out our own special toy and kept expressing gratitude for it.

Our neighbor, George, was over having coffee with my parents one day and observed how excited my brothers and me were playing with our $5 toys. He said, "Wow, I just got my son a $100 toy, and all he did was complain that it was the wrong one and how upset he was that I didn't get him the bigger, more expensive, version. He is in his room pouting about it right now. And here are you guys, playing with $5 toys like they are the best thing in the world. That is incredible."

The difference is gratitude. The more grateful you are, the more things you will discover you have to be grateful for. Maybe something didn't turn out the way you wanted. Perhaps you are going through a rough time, or work with people who are highly toxic. I am not saying it is easy, but I am saying that with a little courage, you can find the treasure or the good in your situation. By doing this, you shift your thinking to a place where you think better, do better, and live better. Be grateful always, and you will always have more to be grateful for.

13

It Takes Courage to Put Yourself First

One of my favorite quotes is, "Don't let anyone make you feel guilty or bad about doing what is best for you."

Recently, I asked a group of leaders, "Who beats us up the most in life?"

In unison, they all replied back, "WE DO!" What do you think?

I think they are right.

What it means to beat yourself up mentally is questioning your worth, doubting your abilities and skills, neglecting your needs, tolerating disrespect from others, carrying the burden of guilt, or making choices that don't serve or add value to your life.

I believe it takes courage to work on yourself, to be kind to yourself, and treat yourself better. Let me give you an example. Recently, I was talking with a good friend, and he said, "Sam, I really struggle with liking myself. I never feel good enough, and I always end up letting the people I love the most down the most. I want to change, but it's so hard. I don't know how to get better."

My encouragement to my friend was not to try and conquer the issue in a day, but to take it one day at a time. And the process of bettering ourselves so we feel better about life is not something we have to do alone. That's why I believe in accountability. Accountability is having someone you trust in your corner who is rooting for you, but also keeps you on track. So, if your goal is to lose thirty pounds, your accountability buddy is going to hold you to achieving that goal. Willpower will only take you so far, and at that point, we need accountability to kick in. Meaning, when you try to skip going to the gym just because you don't feel like it or it's been a long day, whoever is helping you stay accountable to your goal will call you out on your excuse and refuse to let you out of doing what is good for you. They help you get out of your own way. They remove the limitations, which is you making choices that don't move you in the direction of your goal. Accountability is so powerful, and I highly recommend it.

PUT YOURSELF FIRST

Another thing I suggested was to try to make small choices that make you feel better about yourself. Yes, a motivational speaker telling you to "think small." When you accomplish something small that gives your life value, like eating a healthy meal, complaining less, working out, taking a walk after dinner, helping someone out, or working on a new skill, those things make us feel good about ourselves. A small start in a better direction, like changing the words you use to talk to yourself in your mind, can make you feel better about you and life. Think about the words you use daily when you talk to yourself mentally. Are you speaking to yourself with uplifting and positive words, or are you beating yourself up mentally and feeling bad about yourself and life? Do you need to make a change in this department? Remember, you don't always have to do over-the-top big things to feel great about yourself in life. Start small. Start by changing a habit. Start by changing a routine. Start small and gain big!

One of my mentors shared with me years ago, "Sam, when our people work harder on themselves, they become better at what they do." It takes courage to stop, pause, and turn a little focus on bettering yourself and those you care about. I know in my world, my wife and I are always hyper focused on our three kids. So much so that sometimes we forget to take time to focus on ourselves—like connecting, reading a good book, or getting out to have a little free time.

When we had our first daughter, I came home from one of my longer speaking road trips and noticed my wife looked overly exhausted. We were new parents, and sometimes, when you bring your child home from the hospital, they don't like to sleep for a few a years. It's just part of the gig. However, I told my wife, "You gotta go lay down and sleep." Her response was, "I can't, I have too much to do."

I said, "If you are this exhausted, you are not going to be any good for anyone, especially yourself. You have to go rest and take a little YOU time."

Some people feel guilt for doing something nice or necessary for themselves, and I want to encourage you not to feel that or carry that around with you. If someone makes you feel guilty, they have their own bag of issues. If someone is making you feel guilty, you have to ask yourself if they are really rooting for your best interests. Don't listen to or absorb toxic opinions that are geared to prevent you from becoming a better you.

PUT YOURSELF FIRST

Remember, if you are not in a good place, then you are not going to think right, do right, or live right. It's that simple. So, it is fair to say that it takes courage to put yourself first. For example, I know that to be a better dad to my kids or a better husband to my wife, there are things I have to do that focus solely on me—like taking care of my health, making smart choices, or wearing deodorant daily. Basically, you have to take a little time to focus on creating a better you so you think better, do better, and live better. Take time to celebrate yourself, do something that fuels you with energy, fills you with joy and happiness, or gives you a deeper sense of peace and less stress. When you feel better about you, you think better, do better, and live better.

14

It Takes Courage to Be Positively Contagious

Have you ever met someone and because they had such a great attitude, you thought, "I don't know what they had for breakfast, but I want some of it?"

That is what it means to have a positively contagious attitude. Have you ever had a great experience with a company or organization and thought, "I will stick with them forever!" It takes courage to be positively contagious as a person, a company, or a team. It means you have to think a certain way and behave a certain way to achieve that remarkable level of greatness. Greatness is achieved through consistency. It's not a once and a while type of gig, but something that is only grasped through courage, commitment, discipline, and people who care.

As I am writing this chapter at my special writing spot, which happens to be the cafeteria area at St. Vincent Hospital, I can see doctors, nurses, maintenance, support staff, and visitors walking into the dining area to get food. Sometimes, I like to take a break from the keyboard, look up, and observe. I found this little gem of a spot when my wife and I had our kids here. It's a cozy little area where I can focus, relax, and do what I love—write. As I write this, all these people are walking into the dining area to grab some food, and what stands out the most is the attitude of the dining staff. Its impressive. It's contagious! It's courageous! The guy checking people out is telling everyone, "Keep on smiling!"

BE POSITIVELY CONTAGIOUS

From my point of view, everyone is leaving looking a little happier than when they walked in. It could be the really good food they serve there, but I think it's something more. It's people doing what they do in a way that serves others with excellence. The experience they create is positively contagious. I dig that! While the dining staff isn't performing surgery, checking in patients, landscaping, or drawing blood, they are playing their role in a way that makes a difference and contributes to the big picture. It's about recognizing that every role contributes to creating the big picture of success. Success is not possible if everyone is out for themselves, going their own direction, and doing their own thing with whatever the attitude of the day is. That is inconsistent with how you achieve greatness. When everyone is pitching in and contributing the right way, credit is deserved. So let me give some…

What puts a natural and positive light on the big picture of success is when we give credit to each other, respecting that everyone has a role, and each role makes a contribution. The math doesn't work if some contribute in positive way and others subtract in a negative way by creating drama, complaining, not caring, or not giving their best in their role. Success is the recognition that everyone is a priority and brings an element of value to the overall big picture.

If you walk through St. Vincent, just walk into any bath- room—they are always super clean! Think about it, if I am talking about clean bathrooms in a book that is going to be read by people worldwide, what does that say about the quality of work being done in those bathrooms? Whoever is cleaning those bathrooms is doing it with the right attitude. They are playing their role with excellence because those bathrooms are perfect! Trust me, I know. I used to clean bathrooms as a part-time job years ago. Is it a fun job? No way! But not every job is designed to be a joy ride at a fun park. Plus, there are always changing elements to every role. It could be a new policy, new technology, new people coming in, some people going out, understaffing, new roles, new ways of doing things, massive growth, new regulations, and that list can go on and on all day long.

So, you may not have the best of it at your job, but when you add a little courage to what you do, you are empowered to make the best of it. Just because your work may not be filled with a ton of joy doesn't mean you can't experience joy at what you do. Just because the work is not the most ideal isn't a valid reason to let up and get lazy. The moment anyone lets up, gets lazy, and stops caring is the moment the big picture of success begins to fade to dark.

I don't think there has been a single time when I have gone to work on my books at St. Vincent that someone employed there hasn't sent a smile in my direction or greeted me with a little kindness. That is impressive. Credit belongs to their leadership for making this type of culture a priority. You really get the vibe that people work together there, respect each other's roles, and that every role is a big deal. It seems like a place where people can look forward to go to work. That is a big deal.

Whatever industry you work in, this concept applies

to you. To be positively contagious, you have to make a commitment to start each day with the courage to give your best in the role you have and make the best with whatever resources you have.

15

It Takes Courage to Lead in Life

What is interesting about leadership is that it can be demonstrated anywhere at any time by anyone. Leadership is not something that requires permission but rather, a courageous and caring mindset to step up and make a positive contribution. Leadership can be displayed in service, sales, education, administration, hospitality, medicine, safety, retail, housing, software, recruiting, maintenance—you name it. It can be displayed in the home, shopping at the local grocery store, having a difficult conversation with someone, driving in rush-hour traffic, or going for a walk around the block. The capacity of when, where, or how we can demonstrate leadership in life is limitless.

For the most part, a large number of people equate and

confine the concept of leadership to just the workplace;however, leadership encompasses many areas other than the workplace. There are still a lot of leadership opportunities when you pull out of the workplace parking lot. When you grasp this picture, you will understand that leadership is not one-dimensional. It is something that can be applied in many forms, ranging from how we use our attitude, communicate, think, effort, behaviors, and choices. But it is important to acknowledge that all leadership requires COURAGE.

Here are just a few examples of what courageous leader- ship in life looks like:

Courageous leadership is getting yourself out of bed, dressed, and moving when everything inside you wants to quit, call it, and wave the little white flag.

Courageous leadership is the process of doing the best you can with what you have and where you are.

Courageous leadership is the customer service

representative who deals with angry customers all day, yet manages to keep a positive attitude.

Courageous leadership is the entrepreneur trying to make a sale to pay the mortgage and provide for his family.

Courageous leadership is the single mom who takes on extra work or hours to provide for her children.

Courageous leadership is the person battling cancer who still finds ways to encourage and give others courage.

IT TAKES COURAGE TO LEAD IN LIFE

A courageous leader cares and never asks the question, "What is the least I can do to make a difference?"

Courageous leadership is sitting with someone who is depressed and just listening.

Courageous leadership is having those tough and slightly uncomfortable conversations. (You know the kind.)

It takes courageous leadership to hire a motivational speaker to inspire all your employees, knowing full well that inspiration is not something that is easily measured. Without inspiration, our attitudes and actions get burned out and fall flat. (And if you need proof, just ask any organization honored with the title of Best Places to Work!)

Courageous leadership is letting everyone know you care by encouraging them to be safe at work because you want everyone to go home unharmed to their families.

I will stop there, but I bet you could think of some really good examples of courageous leadership in life. The doorway to demonstrating leadership in life is always open to us. We just have to have the courage to care and walk through it. When we apply courage to our personal and professional leadership, we make contributions that change lives for the better and set an example others are excited to follow.

The Wrap Up

As I wrap this little book up, I want to share the same thing I shared when we started—life requires courage. Courage means something unique to each of us. The pur- pose of my work as an author and speaker is to empower people and organizations to think better, do better, and live better. That kind of development is a process of growth that requires courage and consistency. Not every day is going to be a perfect one, but rather, a progressive journey of growth and new adventures that require courage.

I hope the past few pages have encouraged you and also expanded your mental awareness of how valuable living with courage is. If there is one thing for certain, it's that the roots of our courage grow deeper and stronger when we find strength in each other. Never forget that.

If you have a story about courage and want to share it, feel free to email me anytime. (Sam@SamGlenn.com)

Until next time, remember: "Live With Courage!"

Meet the Author

Sam Glenn

Sam Glenn is an award-winning motivational speaker, best selling author, and performance artist. Organizations and leadership teams utilize Sam's uplifting and artistic speeches to recognize, reward and reinforce effort, attitude and achievement. Audiences laugh, learn and experience a moment to recharge and feel good about who they are and what they do.

At one time Sam was negative, depressed and sleeping nights either in his car or on borrowed floor space. It was a good friend, over a cup of coffee, that gave Sam what he calls, "A Kick in the Attitude!" Sam realized that everything follows attitude and that if he wanted his life to change, he needed to start by changing his attitude.

For more than 27 years, Sam has captivated audiences of all sizes, including stadium events up to 75,000 people. Also, Sam's late mentor was the legendary Zig Ziglar.

Today, Sam gives more than 100 speeches a year, working with organizations and leadership teams who really care about the well being of their people.

To book Sam Glenn to speak at your next event, visit: www.SamGlenn.com

Or Email Sam's booking team, Contact@SamGlenn.com